**GOD'S GREAT HEROES**

Four great stories
from the
Old Testament

## CONTENTS

| | |
|---|---:|
| David the Brave | 2 |
| Solomon the Wise | 10 |
| Elijah the Fierce | 16 |
| Samson the Strong | 22 |

Retold from Scripture by Claire Freedman
Illustrated by Arthur Baker

# DAVID THE BRAVE
1 Samuel 17

David was a young shepherd boy. One day, his father met him on the hillside. 'Here's some food,' his father said.
'Take it to your brothers.'

David didn't hesitate. His older brothers were soldiers in the Israelite army. They were fighting their hated enemy, the Philistines. 'I can find out what is happening,' David thought.

As David arrived, the battle was about to start. The Israelites, led by King Saul, were in a terrible state. 'The Philistines have a great warrior on their side,' David's brothers told him. 'He's called Goliath and he's a giant!'

No one dared - only David stepped forward. He knew God was on his side. 'I will fight!' David answered bravely. 'You're too young!' his brothers gasped. But David replied, 'I have killed lions and bears whilst protecting my sheep. God helped me then, he'll help me now!'

King Saul offered David his armour, but it was too heavy for him. Instead, David chose five smooth pebbles from the brook for his shepherd's sling. A big hush fell as David and Goliath stood face to face.

'You fight with weapons,' David shouted at Goliath, 'but I fight in the name of God!'

Using his sling, David aimed a pebble at Goliath's head. It hit, and with an almighty 'CRRRASH!' Goliath dropped down dead! The cheers in the Israelites' camp were deafening!

# SOLOMON THE WISE
1 Kings 3

David became King of Israel, and his son Solomon ruled after him. One night, God appeared to King Solomon in a dream.

'What do you wish from me?' God asked. 'O Lord,' Solomon replied, 'you have made me king and I want to serve you. Give me wisdom so I can govern your people well. Show me right from wrong!'

God was pleased. 'Because you have asked nothing for yourself,' God said, 'I will give you great wisdom, and riches and honour besides. You will be the greatest king that ever lived!'

Solomon's wisdom was soon put to the test. Two women came to him, one carrying a baby. 'O King!' the first woman cried. 'This other woman and I live together. We both had baby boys. During the night this woman's baby died as she lay on it. While I slept, she swapped her dead baby for mine. Now she says my baby is hers!'

Then the second woman shouted, 'No, the baby is mine! It is hers that died!' King Solomon asked for a sword. 'Cut the baby in two and give each woman a share,' he said. What a terrible thing to say!

But only the first woman tried to save the child. 'Don't kill him!' she begged. 'Let the other woman keep him!' Then Solomon said, 'The first woman has proved she is the real mother - give her the baby!'

All who heard were amazed at Solomon's wise judgement!

# ELIJAH THE FIERCE
1 Kings 18:16-40

Israel had good and bad kings, but Ahab was the most evil. He and his wife Jezebel hated God. They worshipped an idol called Baal instead.

After three years of drought, Elijah visited Ahab again. Ahab was not pleased to see him! 'You've caused Israel's trouble!' Ahab accused. 'No!' replied Elijah, 'your wickedness has!'

Elijah ordered Ahab to gather the people together at Mount Carmel. When they arrived Elijah demanded, 'Who is the true God - Baal or God?' No one answered. 'Right!' Elijah shouted, 'let us both prepare a bull for sacrifice, one to Baal and one to God. The one who can send down fire to burn the sacrifice is the true God.' So the people prepared their bull.

'O Baal, answer us!' the priests of Baal called, dancing around their altar, but nothing happened! Then came Elijah's turn. He was so certain of God that he even poured water over his altar!

God had a plan for Samson even before he was born, so he sent an angel to Samson's mother to tell her. 'You will have a son,' the angel said. 'By his amazing strength he will destroy Israel's enemy, the Philistines! But he must never cut his hair, or his strength will go!'

Samson was born and he grew up to be super strong! Once, Samson killed a thousand Philistines in one day, just by using the jawbone of a donkey! The Philistines feared Samson. 'What is the secret of his strength?' they wondered.

In time, Samson fell in love with a woman called Delilah. The Philistines went to her and said, 'Discover what makes Samson so strong and we'll pay you one thousand pieces of silver!'

Delilah agreed. Day in, day out, she pestered Samson, saying, 'Tell me your secret!' Finally Samson told her. 'I have never cut my hair. If my head were shaved, my strength would go!'

While Samson slept, Delilah had his hair cut off. As arranged, the Philistines came for him. 'I'll fight them,' thought Samson, but this time he was powerless - his strength had gone!

Samson was blinded and thrown into prison. Soon after, the Philistines brought him into their temple. 'How weak Samson is now!' they mocked. But Samson's hair had grown again!

'O God,' he prayed. 'Give me enough strength to destroy my enemies.'

Samson lent against the temple pillars. He pushed with all his might. CRASH! The temple collapsed. The Philistines all died, and Samson too.

## ............................ THE IMPORTANT!
(Write your name here)

You don't have to be Brave, Wise, Fierce or Strong to be important to God. You already are!

If you love God and try to follow him, you'll always be great in his eyes!

Three cheers for ................................. the Important!

(Write your name here)

31

First published in 1998 by
KEVIN MAYHEW LTD
Rattlesden
Bury St Edmunds
Suffolk IP30 0SZ


© 1998 Kevin Mayhew Ltd


The right of Claire Freedman to be identified as the author
of this work has been asserted by her in accordance
with the Copyright, Designs and Patents Act 1988.

All rights reserved. No part of this publication may be reproduced,
stored in a retrieval system, or transmitted, in any form
or by any means, electronic, mechanical, photocopying,
recording or otherwise, without the prior
written permission of the publisher.

0 1 2 3 4 5 6 7 8 9

ISBN 1 84003 199 9
Catalogue No 1500223


Front cover designed by Jonathan Stroulger
Illustrated by Arthur Baker
Typesetting by Louise Selfe
Printed and bound in Great Britain